SERENADE

SERENADE

BROOKE ELLSWORTH

Octopus Books   Portland   Seattle   Denver

SERENADE

BY BROOKE ELLSWORTH

© COPYRIGHT 2017

ALL RIGHTS RESERVED

PUBLISHED BY OCTOPUS BOOKS

OCTOPUSBOOKS.NET

DISTRIBUTED BY SMALL PRESS DISTRIBUTION

SPDBOOKS.ORG

ISBN 978-0-9861811-6-0

FIRST PRINTING

COVER PHOTOGRAPH © GREGORY HURCOMB

DESIGNED BY DREW SCOTT SWENHAUGEN

2.

3.

SERENADE

FLOWER

There's always a baby in the air
full of idiot alarms

I call it a sunset
I call it a literal armament

lodged in by another person

I'm talking to a sunset with
an arm like that
That is a Hiroshima

I felt the equivalent

information in waves of broke suns
leaking like money
I was son to the yammering sunset
What a deep thrill
I said what an honor to see
your science

and what it takes
to witness the lavation

that exits from the metal

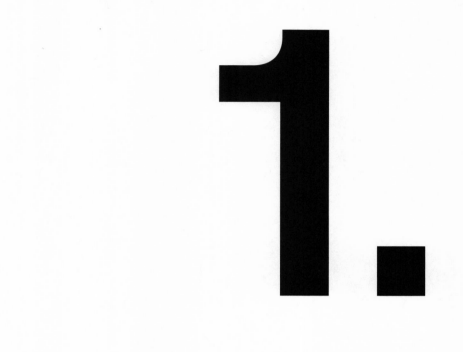

DRUNK TATTOO

My dreams bear witness to
themselves, cheaters
My dreams bear witness to
my relic ham, sad brother
My dreams are submitted
to the newsfeed
Wait hold my glasses and my phone
Wait, my dog soars
up into stability
You are sunk into your mouths
One structure rubbed against another

TRANSPARENCY

Spent days staring at nothing so my language describes nothing or my
language constructs nothing instead of the

> glittering
> blue
> weekends
> The first
> cry of the day
> to empty the
> way for my
> full life
> It would
> have
> to be me
> I hereby apologize
> for the
> price
> of slipping
> With such amounts
> of happiness
> I need more
> happiness
> There is so much
> teeth in
> telling
> a family

I was born
this way
They look out to the
stand
of trees
or over the foggy beach

JOKE

I fill the bed with blood. You're a liar you text back. ha no you're right, I wake
up this parody and I want myself so bad

You text back I wake up this parody. ha no you're right I don't miss anything,
this mopey hamlet in me leaking a love a love

You texted back days later, some serious bathos like shitty
vodka or ex-boyfriends. A love a love

Some days there's so much to love explains the boy in me

THE ICE STORM

My level mind, my new hard-drive, my hypomanic bot
riding the blue
                ha this palace
of stolen Popov. Here's a
natural home to work
as you see bees behind the glass hive
High praise
from the sober audience
calling for the mutt that let out:
Beware Beware
You're like a big annoying door-bell
at this party grrr baby baby
I thought I'd be more or at least capable
of the first sunrise
as you lower into the ice
What does it mean to stand for nothing
A nothing allotted to you
as I turn to you,
you, the lowered glacier,
I have finally rooted
my breath
in your lengthening stain
                erected
                against the Atlantic
                as its critical
                shadow

Always in caves / in moonbeams
the spirit was drest
Hey I'm here
a vision standing over you
dying between each green light

DEATHDREAM

After the hurricane, after the gray. I repeat: blue grass. What I want is to get to know you. Standing hunched and bored there maybe. Texting me on a beach.

There's something so object
about it
and anger
The surf break that could be interpreted
as Annabel Lee
floating along a pitch-black cliff and into the Pacific
I am so glad
    in the Santa Ana winds
tying knots in my hair
The recital is deep enough
to feel like a choice
When I was born I was adjacent to the crystal blue ocean
A boy from the good
old earth
Find your silence I text
the ruined neighbor
The concealed exhaust-
ion for the
crystal to show
in the boyish climes
the
blue

hole
slowing
The wordplay
makes its need
louder

THE RAVING ONES

Pilled out staring at your home screen. A private Act 1: I am a liar, I change,
but I cannot die. I mean who could be

> the aguey strings that
> tighten
> with every
> table
> I've taken under me
> inching closer to obscurity
> in the upshot
> Is that what you want

Would u believe I was sober when I typed in
maenad killer bitch gif
into the browser

> I retire from life every time
> Los jovenes mentiras
> in the summer
> in the summer
> we're all going to the same place, sure
> back to the refrain
> What the flight attendant says
> We couldn't experience
> our gashes
> bc their distortion

blocked the way
and opened the way
to Orpheus' skull
that we studied and
grew to love at
viral levels
My relic
          stands still there
in the light we stand still here
to wife
the intermission

EVICTION

The head of the primal tiger glared out at me in the flattening commercial space. Wine tastings take us into these nasty elevators, spoken for narrowness. The sun is "crazy" and boosted. A build-up of thunderheads

      here in blue
      summer: a panic
      bombshell of meaning
      that cannot be fixed
      My thing is that I'm like unreasonable
      like your hellpain only functions
      on ordered
      porches I grew up
      in a pine tree at night
      right in front of you
      Heartfelt hair-growth
      behind the paywall
      "Hey"
           this is Peter Greenaway
      trying to figure out where to live
      as the camera pans to high ground
      Intestine track
      in a deep comedy
      Peter Greenaway says:
      "I don't know much about you
      You were conceived"
      etc.

You can't just call the people you
want to talk to
You want redwoods
to detect thoughts not emerging out
of crisis
I'm at a party
where everyone's dressed up like Peter Greenaway
and then he gets rolled out
on a big platter
with a big Red Delicious
apple in his mouth
See me love my apology
Everybody wins
whatever they can populate
gull brain

FLORIDA, MASSACHUSETTS

The man behind the counter says no, he's not from around here but he's lived
here long enough he might as well be. Night vision, he then says. You can see
where this is going

             (funeral-ready)
             When they determine me
             When they board me
             up
             We spray-painted gold the
             VFW lawn
             hard with champagne
             You can count on this
             like when you share a poet
             you want to
             say yeah
             sure
             You are here
             to describe yourself
             in relation
             to a
             child all up in the grass
             like a bible
             against the
             invasive
             common reed
             I'm in love with

your subject
matter
I live on your lawns
I live with a
vision
I am quoting a long-lost love poem
I alone
in bible speak
go down with it
in ships

LIFESEND

The golden fowl start first thing, my whole life depends on you, as I arrange a litany like peach pits lined up on the porch to dry [...] threaded into a torc

The network of *Historia Animalium* the animal that runs alongside human invention. This is what

> anachronistic

> Me trying to turn you on

> I am chicken mad

> As I write the uk prime minister is suspected of having ordered destruction of journalist's hard drives

> What more would you know about me if you knew my fantasies (going to Hell with my dog) [...] My, the summer drags

SEPTEMBER, DISSENTS

I step on the train, muted. Like an intrusion of chopped basil. One you want to be like oh hi family this was supposed to be kept from you.

Remember the images of the droughts, a childhood developed by default. They both carried

guns, she said, in the silvergrass behind the subdivision. Hear them take down the length of the moon made of immunity.

The question of how we live after death is not a new one

DYING JOKE

The writing is too small, she said

and lifted her mouth from his belly in the median strip, as though
a squatted coywolf, mothered

Life pouring out, pouring out,
to tell me my wrong mess I saw with such clarity

Sister, I conceived of the production that facilitated my love for
you

Looked up from the shoulder and there was the satellite blowing the shipping
containers off course

Sister
        your beast runs deep

I am the wrong person

Can I salute all you give me

ROOSTER ROCK

The late summer riverbed flattens under our feet

        as we walk along the
        obvious
        mud
        that can't be learned
        This is about
        the rest
        Rooster Rooster
        Whoever dies
        first
        must be eaten
        we promise
        each other
        and then run
        back into
        the Columbia
        River

THESIS

With a body as a house, a darkening house of low-tide astonishment, the
seagull dropping the clam. The idea that carries off the protagonist

> My self-rule vanishes in the haze of
> The hilly redoubt in the bath of
> I have to be in love or else fail under the arm-strength of
> thunders, it
> *thunderbeing*
> When seen from the back
> has no head
>   like a parking lot
> (without record)
> so the common English offers
> a tautology? A plaque? Language as a puce
> gas we are born in and out of in rapid
> oscillation
> Love is a torpefied tree
> A lifestyle rooted in two centuries
> of sadness
> A totally useless forest
> floor of brown leaves
> Historic mud that glows in the throat like hot coals
> Climb down
> my rabid bird your story is so heartless
> your heartless narrative
> of resemblance

My beautiful day
you leave your
head like a thesis
braced
above the body

WATER HOUR

"Visits of drowned joiners to
these
submerging words:"

PAUL CELAN

I forgot to eat again today
and will forget tomorrow
Water Hour

I line up the fish you catch
and put rocks
at their tails for exclamation
points

Today I'm going for the way
erosion chooses its objects
Never asked you where
our cruelty travelled

The stupidest question you get
is if you're lonely

Of course you were
until a hiker
tripped over your stove-pipe sticking out of the hill
and dug out from the topsoil roof
a tube attached to a jug for a shower

A rubber membrane glossed by flashlights
The precedent

for the direct message

1) Big Island
2) Catskills
3) Squam Swamp
4) Atlanta

FUCKING ISLAND

I can go home in the winter and be totally impersonal
Fuck you, sand
I can just scream it
for like an hour
Some guy tied up his famous girlfriend and stabbed her to
death in a big empty mansion
In the winter
mansions either
fall off the cliff or they just move the property back
a movement
that is clearly privileged like
how can you argue against wind turbines as visual pollution
or land
value
When
I read a moral poem
"Whenever Ueno-san says *poetry*, it sounds like
death," —Hiromi Itō
My fucking beautiful ocean
My ocean is moral

LIFE IS BEAUTIFUL

I was drinking purse wine in gridlock
on the George Washington when I got yr
email
Don't come back
and suddenly I felt smoked out like diesel
the smoke just lifting into a holiday
that is so pleasant in
the performance
Lifted into a landscape painting of a blasted tree
A blessed blankness
A bright sun
You psycho
You enter the lonely
farm-house
What sun do you worship
I keep shouting down the train
when it rains
When it rains
the tunnels flood
and we romantics
multiply
Ahorita, a gift of happiness
Milky Way, a gift of happiness
In this open world, a gift of happiness,
we flood in private

FURIOUS LENGTHS

Toils as much as I can on all fours, low branches. I opened the hatch and thought, "Oh, my God."

Thought I'd take to the watery part of the world driving off the spleen into tar pits of *what of it*

What of the shitwork that spills over our crude mattress

Where does it collect

THE SUN ENTERED THE ROOM WITH THE LIST OF ITS YELLOW LIGHT

I lifted my skirts in horror, lifted the mouth of my haunting into a realism

My young itch

Watching a funeral procession from the window in my shower I begin to clap

for the opposite motorcade
hunnn hunnn hunnn

RITZ NAILS

In this kind of going dark
I am going to plays
I have no idea why I'm there, what license pulls the center

        Going crazy is a type of
        gravity, sure
        if you listen
        to the house
        stupid
        with
        death
        The rules of the
        playhouse are
        1) deaf and 2) enter into
        the Gulf
        of Mexico and enter into
        the inky
        fish
        3)
        the poem
        empties
        4) from above I paint the empty
        house

EROS

Nay further, we are what we all abhor, Anthropophagi and Cannibals, devourers of not onely men, but of ourselves; and that's not just in an allegory, but a positive truth / Just the other night for example I found the receipt I threw away from the Emergency Room / A kiss for luck!

You drew a circle around
your mouth
as I answered emails
to answer
yes
yes
yes
Sir,

look
He put a hand
to his leg
shadow
a childhood
of reversed-
reaching into
tide pools
Able-bodied in
1643,
a blurred
spleen

Some dreams
are worth the
monotony
of love
[...]
the snow
turns the
block
white
I believe you
yes
yes
yes

VICKI YOU'RE A DEAD MAN

which is more like seeing baby pictures of yourself, does anybody ever really
know

Vicki sees
some guy who works for the local network sitting there

then he's lecturing about adult responsibility. I know how to love and work.
But you gotta tell me what to do because I'm a liar.

Showing up was Mistake #1
You start out with a subject

and then choke on delivery. You think about O'Hara and how ambiguous her
mind becomes

looking at this life as the public domain song, bc they're both pretty bullshit,
once you peel back the orange and drop it from the window

Call me when you figure out who you are

She never started out as a human being
Is nothing to you
Did nothing to encourage
your likes

O'Hara: Vicki, you're a dead man

AFTERLIFE

I quit
smoking
because it started to trigger
migraines
Like
a garbage
truck
and I'd
have my
head
on
my knees
There's no real
reason
I started
besides the
excuse
to
stand there and
stare
across
the
road
stand
over
cold

horses
I stand over my head
and
slip
into
the
poem
that is
the
crowd

EXPANSIONISM

See I'm
sitting here
on the
train
crying
a really good
cry
bc who the fuck
knows
So like
I'm looking at some
phone
some kind of orange shiny
food on some spinach
Drinking With Cousins
I have no
idea
what irony
is
In workshop once
we were
reading this poem
I just couldn't help
it
saying "my sweet sweet"
repeatedly

The Sapphic stanza
naked in the wind
Read it like 3 fists to the mirror
An example of irony somebody
says
and I'm like
by what
rules
do
I cut my own
hand

FLACA

Two burned masks, there are two of me. I'm eating garnish and can be
encased in the pleasure, set sail. Hey you I estrange in a deadness, which is
of necessity. I turn around to nothing, to the heroin self-evidence. I am on
fire with myself. Touch my dick and I touch the ghost of my dick. I advise the
newsfeed

        with the razed mountain of ash
        and the Gatsby
        that was razed
        along with it
        Skinny bitches
        from which their source
        is themselves
        Somebody
        found a screw
        in their black beans
        A screw
        like hand me the screwdriver
        Up in Alaska
        everybody works for Aramark
        so this is common
        one of the bartenders tells
        me
        He loves
        meat
        He's been a

junkie
forever
I have been circling
Years later I saw
his profile
picture
him and
some
girl holding a
gun on a
boat
I enter the heart
I am
hungry
for
myself

SOLAR FLARES

Solar flares gain momentum the further they travel from their source, like being surrounded by hubris on the end of a 13-hour day

Your mouth tastes like shit, yes, bc it's been that long since you brushed yr teeth

      What is touching me

      in my doubting
      brain

      Yessir

ERASERHEAD

I'm thinking about the dead seal again

This is one
pissed off rock
I thought as
I leaned
closer
Come
and look at
this rock
I said
then followed
you back to the
dead seal
I am a dead roof
Look you
said
and held out
a piece of
its spine
I am a
man
dragging
a wheelchair

DEEPWATER HORIZON

Awash with the freedom to not say whatever
on my back kind of
glancing over the surface of the sea
of my cruelty
with the browsing motion of reading
Birds glide in

my mouth
She is so nice
not to miscarry the statue
What roots in the company

The videos of the ones who identify with their own imagery
(New York hurricanes)
(Waking life under Breton's Paris)
(Drivers on the hard shoulder)

They are arguing for your terminal, terminal

Nobody is ever totally out
but beautiful things happen when we rotate as though we could
press on the tail of each other's lips

Thinking about our political failure to respond
to the ecological crisis, there are cushions in the air
that I faced with my opening

oblivious to the informal answer
"Robert sat in a chair under a black-and-white Larry Rivers"
I read over a boy's shoulder and think about the blurred
roofs that move across the sound

The albatross of this catastrophe being the garbage albatross
slicing thru the dirt
I am alone

Reading, even in its most
foglike state
is never invisible

To live alone one has to be a beast Nietzsche summarizes Aristotle

and are my new beasts sounded out
My authority, reader, is that I am illegible like an oil-shale mine spreading
its shaky legs

Image:
It wasn't an albatross it was a
pragmatism

I paid to listen with the luxury of a student

Call me Warm Ocean / when you embody me
A garbage confession
Listening to standards /
Standard

A warm ocean on a Saturn moon rises in the bed next to me
I say out of industry

There's always a writing reflected in the real world
I say out of industry

From between my legs there is a tar, managed
thru research thru your research
Bragging on the albatross, ragging on
the end-sound
You are braced

but who is the one effaced

in the elegy

I'M STUPID IN THIS HOUSE

Grabbed the tree and grabbed the tree's
fence
to look about the military camp
I am saying here is the park
circulating in
the symbolic space

I guess I was recording in a
base way, like here's an intro to the
very sorry ontology
Today feels so real
Memorial Day is the most real day
A superlative point
this nature
among other natures

I've been fantasizing about my hands
dipped into the brine of my childhood
a symbolic gloss of performance

The world is alive
with credulity

That which exists obviously

that is seen as the red tide bloom
and is seen as the under-fiction
What birds don't eat
What theoretical fingers don't
dip into the large, tangle of wires

I take from here the emptying sounds of paradise
but it is to be exchanged

I take from here the emptying sounds of paradise
but it is then an appearance
of a bird or a flag

My ugly head lowers to the grass
I'm not sorry I choose to focus on the logic
of your real estate, the lines of skin that form your aging
eye

I fear nature

I fear the birds that drag
the material world
out of me

I know how to live in this universe

I know when to cover my hair
in sand

THE EMPTY LOTS IN
THE MOVIE OF MY LIFE

My stupid winters are full of abstract jobs like visit the desert or
don't visit the desert
This Planet Is Doomed by Sun Ra

What if this sun was the end of your life
My ego emerges from your torso

I retire from life
every time I beg for more
Beatrice

I die for private thoughts
I die for tongueless drivers
to just sit there and wait for me to
finish crying

The empty lots in the movie of my life
look over the expanding lawns
and to the left
the Badlands are veined
with lightning

I comb the leaves from your hair and I oil your feet with complete gratitude
for this world rooted onto your back

In our young nests
we produce mantras for the retention ponds
Is that what you want to hear

I hate that you watch whatever video is on your newsfeed

and then tell me about it

I hate that I have to imagine some other way of wasting my life

It's so easy getting pregnant, but to accumulate vision

    Maybe
    sleep only stuns
    with its advantage
    when we turn
    away
    during its
    assembly

NEAR FANTASY

The photograph: A gilded circuit found in the core of the most exquisite snowflake

> The core of the
> day
> discharged
> from the stem
> I am loyal to my
> fuel as I cart around my cunt
> A big
> shrieks & grease hunt
> Please, stay still there in
> the pool of light
> Stay still there
> This family isn't
> going
> to forget
> itself

SERENADE

"I am a limitless series of natural disasters."

KATHY ACKER, *PUSSY, KING OF THE PIRATES*

Grounded for finger-fucking, we took our without-airplane hands to the
setting. Wanting

desire
itself
to align like
trees
down the neigh
borhood
The shadow and the
bear
The energy
of collapse
Up at dawn
a disaster moving
toward
a past
2014 is
right
in front of
me
and the 2014 wind
is picking

up
my cancer
puss
my
natural
home
here in 2014
I climb up a
bunker
built for a Kennedy
something I did as
a girl
when
it was a lot
further
from the
cliff
Innovation
bores
in fits of billions
you
are
one
It goes without saying
to feel the
conclusion
hanging its garden
I write
for you
and I write
for the

knowledge
of anonymity
as we roll out
the century
in a
rented
ocean
texting
old
numbers
Wrong person
they finally
send
Wrong
person
sometimes
you gotta
keep
the
conversation
going

2.

&

Wherever I stand

I am the center of space

Like you sit down
expecting to title the movement
Annihilation

You move no cloud

You move
me

A global fallacy

&

Where did this mountain come from

I am
insane

Doctors you have been outmoded

I replaced my brain with my dead ass

There are pigs like me that wallow
There are pigs like me that wallow in their destiny

I ate my parents
and gave birth to nothing

The house where I lived is strange to me

FAKE TREE

Fake tree
stop giving birth
to me

Fake tree

when people tell me I have your hair
when people tell me I have your hair
it feels real

like the elevator opens
for nobody

like you hate me
Stop filling me with gentle
hate

Tree of shit yr mistakes are showing

To those here to invent
a law

is this everybody's ruin

to inflate

THE GOLDEN YEARS

Cats n girls
cats n girls / having something to do with sickness
my baby fist leans into the white
sleep
scattered over a desk like loose almonds pulled from a bag
An eroding new england
Hey family debt family sleeping at night
I wanna be the dinner

RED

You're painting again I can tell by the way you grab my ankle
just like when I can tell you dream about me lying to you

for whom I was debilitated by a second market
until I folded over its licit
being

Could I throw it all open under the pine

I heard that song

I said not until u decide who is crazier u or me

I felt a schizophrenic trigger in our confluence of interests

Who's crazier
all the people I love

I live thru them
Who are we
I recall

you as a rational language

RED

Washing down decongestants with cold coffee reading yr glistening
        emails
just a free-floaty fragment without a torso

as if what I was possessed by was your missing arm
reaching south of the fragment

The cow-dog lifts its appetite skyward
in a clear beginning of overcrowding

Took out my phone and asked who's there

2015 IS DEAD

I guess it's too late to live on the farm
bc I'm a baby

I'm also starving
for positivism

Later I'll post about how we're really just talking mud
Today was okay

I retain in me a shred of muddiness
I'm giving birth to the old world

I'm living in the old love
feeling for everybody

GOOD NEWS

The years that pass

remember the dead one we threw
over the highway

he loved to ride
in cars

I'm talking about the dog

keep the dog in
Bears are in the trash again

near the Christmas tree
under the porch

I'll have no chance to wipe flies
from my brother's face

the mass
on the waterlogged trees

but I knew when
a visible getting off

from the interstate
wherever
the difference bottled

is living thru some shit

Family bleeding out

What is it to yield a thing

and clown its dreams
I am a clown

under your dog

I dog

under your dog

What is it to age and to feel

it

I need you to know I had to do something

The feeling stays a stretched, blue skin
even when we fail
This is a society

I'm not working
to fix things

In the armed trees
I found in the daytime
my funeral

at the end of the cord
as I came over the rise

Passport

What pre-existing forms enter
that we still carry inside

A wild blue movie

Algal blossoms

Nihilism

You can't get rid of the ground
Not true anymore
You can check under my hair again

I want to do the work

The activism that leaks from the screen
lights my cigarette

not in a generally
famous way

but adjacent to my rage

Love my talent for being awful

Love as a possession

sprays over the cluster
of mangroves

We were raised isolated

would bury the dog in pillows

with an opening at the top

the size of my head

meant only for my head

Visualize
journalism

There is wind

There is red

that drips down
the dream
of being anybody else

I was jealous

of my own captivity

is it that I was a fuck-up
born

on top
of a reef

Dreams

are where I dump my forms

There is only one source

Accident drives these planes

By accident

the bad planes that drizzle

to earth

Make us

Whose legs are not the inverse of the cost
that growls in my heart

I'm a liar

I tell you I am

so mindless

with art

3.

DEAR KILLING NARCISSUS

Dreaming my life away today, sitting in your pine tree. I woke up and walked down to the riverbed feeling like I was writing you. Feeling like we ducked into the shade against a big brick wall refreshing the newsfeed. Angry and sweating. Do we get some coffees, I asked no one just to feel like I was thinking ahead. *At what point is it controversial to write my death is inevitable*, you yelled. In the empty fields, we come alive. It could be about thinking ahead. Ghost-bed, *I could feel every pore, I yearned for every pore.* I could feel the rotting already. What if it was your pine tree. You could go about your business knowing I was there, expressing me there, and once in a while glancing out a window, you'd see me like two clouds covering the hills.

Everything looks at everything. When I am dead nowhere. No human is a stadium (we don't know) or the construction of a displacement. What happens when life is a bag. Who knows. Life is already a bag. You know how I hate empiricism. I almost never leave my room. I am saying this because I'm beginning to love you I don't want to see you anymore. Kathy Acker interviewed Spice Girls and said it's up to them and people like them to "keep on transforming society as society is best transformed with lightness and in joy."

LUNCH IS SERVED ON THE PATIO

We are on the bed in front of a fan listening to the restaurant downstairs.
You don't understand is what I say and I really mean it. Like you're a memoir
clogging my inbox. A second anchor pulling at my fight. I am always greedy
for an end. I respect the extra words

that have nothing to do with my target. Dislodged like the entire flock of
starlings as they whip through the trees. Starlings are the men of birds. The
objective end to the talking. I'm at the writing's limit, a dislocated anger. It
has an orange middle.

WE TRAVEL TO READINGS THRU
SELF-STORAGE HIGH-RISES

Why can't the important things be what I have always known. Like your shoulders when we are swimming and later I write behind your back *you are exposed.* I lift my harm, small, above my waist

and later after some thought I throw my phone in the trash. A painless memory widening like a pool of saliva. I come out of the city and lean into the window as the train glides under the off-ramps like a wrong intimacy. Airless tunnels of art. The jurisdictions pushed outside of the argument.

Soon my image of you merges with an image of Nancy Bush by her sister's side. A totally unnecessary account but it all comes together anyway. Not a move toward minimalism, but maybe a similar Beckett-move of flipping destitution on its head. A flower! *No lyric has ever stopped a tank.* And yet I know the sun

came up and we stumbled out of the river, silver with cold fog. I was such a failure. To this, the reduction aimed its recovery. Its breathing in the deviation.

THE PAIN OF DIALOGUE

The call comes in waves. Placing the right hand over my ribs, slowly towing down. To remind me I'm not authoring the poem. I lift my shirt in the mirror to see the expanding bone. Eelgrass submerged by the force of a thesis

a building that was stopped short in the remote field. Circling like an annotation. I want to save my obsession with you (eel). I can do it without lying, I can create on top of your life. Do you see how this song discharges. He says you're no machine / He says this ATM can drive its own screen. Its red summer battery set soft on the trail. Its surface set in its own right. Its redress set as I drag the code thru the gorge.

THE SKY'S DARK BLUE CHARITY

Echo smokes a lot and saves the butts. She writes a lot of poems and posts them on her Myspace accounts (2003). She has the deleterious pattern of creating profiles, uploading content, to then deactivate them after a few weeks. This anti-archival proclivity maybe comes out of a childhood of ecological anxiety. In this way, written seriously, pleasure is a thought on a cold beach. We have to back each other up.

Laughing down the dirt roads behind the school, Echo and Narcissus collect used smokes in the front pocket of her backpack for later. They hide when boys walk by, waiting for their hollering to fade. *We will never die*, Narcissus whispers to Echo's stomach as they lie on their backs in the tall grass, watching Venus rise from the horizon. Later Echo wakes in the dark covered in dew. She stands up then finds her way home.

HOLED UP / ECHO'S SCENE
OF ECOLOGICAL BETRAYAL

In the duration of the gaze you become a pool of headiness. I am spellbound, as I gather my shells and ash. I don't wonder for an end to the melting glaciers, I wonder that I can form their surface and sleep in their mouths. To write about the opposition of the present is to write about the bodies preserved in the bog. This is more convincing, squatting in front of the chorus. *I almost love you*, I say as I turn to face the sagebrush sweeping the hill. I take off my shirt and throw it into the pond and then I throw whatever hair I can pull from my beard. I strive to enter you into the bog by striving to enter myself.

> Having become a cannibal, she does not drag her own species behind her, having dreamed

> of the submergence. The censorship. Could anything be felt in the omission, the turnstile event of monstrosity, there is no general point

> but a mess of contingencies

> The fact is big

OUR IMAGE OF HAPPINESS
IS INDISSOLUBLY BOUND
TO THE IMAGE OF USE

I am so fired

when Narcissus comes together as a group. They all listen when the woman
speaks. They see the opening vent.

> I never met a single person
> I never learned to say *I hear you*
> Don't you see yourself in anything
> Easy reading
> Throwing it all over the bar
> Did u pass me on the interstate / railing
> that separated pond from more pond
> I want it to be 10 years ago
> I want it to be 2004
> I want it to be 2003
> I want it to be 2002
> I want it to be 2001
> I want it to be 2000
> Say hullo mom
> Say hullo dad
> I see a killing forest in 2004
> I'm beside the road
> I'm unlucky

In 2003 I felt alive
just prior to gathering my thoughts
as I pull into the dead bell
I pull under her ribs

I AM MY OWN DREAM /
I AM MY OWN DREAM

What is familiar that grows on trees. "Send me a shirt, towel, trousers, reins, and for my sister, send fabric," written in Old Novgorod on birch bark. Wikipedia calls it "magical mud." If I am alive, I will pay for it. I, beast. I *waited*. I *waded*. In the burden, the preservation of the undermining of fog. I asserted that there is enchantment. I waded into the fermentation. This is the everyday, the wet center of hating. I want you, and you want me. I remember the year 1030. I remember because you studied the tree in my mouth, one, two, tree

(the wet center is bottomless) the dream is of remote shelling. Tree roots overgrow the development and it dreams (the tree), this shelling, remote in time

as the tree dreams, so does a heart: In Huntington Beach, the World Cup, in Camp No, in no expenditure, the opening ceremony, in assembly.

ECHO / NARCISSUS

Tree entwined with the general Instagram appreciation for the balance of the frame.

The blasted tree, disrupting, dialogue tree of moving bark. The birch tree. The bog tree.

Tree that hangs over you like a lake. Tree that grows from the back.
You can go to hell, you ugly messenger floating over me like an object (feels so blessed), this could be a threat. I lay there and imagined I was completely loved, the tiny baby that bled out of my nose

while using the presidential we
The we that is returned to the realty
The we that could delegate the task downward
The coywolf we that steals thru yr neighborhoods
or not the we but the muscle that extends, our troubled ears, turned seriously
toward the high humming that is an interior collaboration
in the wind that blows like I'm 90 yrs old
said the conspicuous paperwhite form
Downwar
Downward
Come on, to my house
and get me on my young house

ENTRY TEXT / REMOVAL TEXT

Kiss and ride

Echo in the act of diminishment loses the referent (if the record exists of it
ever possessing the referent). A process that mimics waste

and is rooted in soil. A process of accumulation, of generation and
degeneration. Addition, accumulation. Possession by way of containment
and extinction. Echo is complete faith in this process.

Her bones, they say, are transformed into stone.

BARK

My cunts dropped into the ground. A brood of cicadas into the ground. I see a mad choreography in the cell: I sweat out buildings. In what source. I want to look and see the concept embedded in the home. What dropped from the dog in the tree. Dog in the tree, don't it hurt a little / to be so close to the gut you were meant to be. Aaaiiiiyyy don't know. What I came from in here. And what dropped out of the pond was a version of our fuck army. And what could art dog into besides that surface. I am bored reading anybody but myself.

At night I swap out legs. They are less ready than the previous ones, which is to be expected. At night I call it a corpse to end all corpses. I need the light more than I admit. Two-legged stridulating, and the marshes that discharge from the breaks in the exterior. Or the flimsy skin of our rights, reconfigured analogously to the spatial relations of the city. Anyway you know how I love to watch.

You asked me once if I could ever love anything more than myself

Do you remember asking me that

The tree whose name means bang

Mama Dada, I said,

what I wouldn't give
to drink out of your luster chalice

Loving someone is not possible

What was melting, you asked

July is a woman
July sucks out my object
as I read Anna Kavan's *Ice* in the southern light of the bedroom

Is it possible there is such a rational plan
Is it possible that I could grow out of my ice sea
I could have been reading anything
It's July on the Hudson

Is it possible to read a book and embody the author. Well what you need
to know is that I read *Ice* and I was the author Anna Kavan in the reading.
The sky is gray, grayer clownish buildings towering against it. A smoldering
begins to bloom on the buildings. I pick out where I see a shapeless yellow
body against the gray from the corner of my left eye. I'm looking thru the
corner of my eye. It was the end of a cigarette lodged into my hair. The man
keeps walking, hooting and screaming. Why this token, feels right. Part of the
piling up of bewilderment I guess I feel. Bewilderment, but I feel no surprise.
Walking down the sidewalk freezing and wet I jam my fingers into my hair,
choking on the sizzling. I shake it loose from the now scorched patch on the
left side of my head and continue to turn in that direction, the direction of
my burnt hair toward the train. At once I see myself there, in that crooked
pitch pine in the dirt driveway. Somebody's mom would walk out her door
and look up at me sitting there completely unsurprised I was there. This look!
Didn't she want to know why I was there. Where was her son. Did she know.
Did she know me. Who was I to sit in her tree.

I employed the conflation of memory to open the flower
We must think of spring

We poets know negation
is impossible bc it requires capital
but its adjacent codes
accrue
sometimes aesthetic
On workers comp
you texted and said you were going to carry me to the bar
bc my foot was broken
and then we drank and you carried me back and there was this
Cadillac convertible
on the sidewalk with its top town
It was so warm out
so we got in it and fucked for a while
before I got mad
and limped home

Sources could merge as if to jaundice

the day I meet my brain brought up from the pipeline. *Fill us up with the outside.* I'm ready here for big and beautiful things. The very sands that insist on its yield. A useful marrow, although the extraction is subcontracted.

A dumping out of green light
as I faced the document
against the teeth

Is this mastery

to produce a Victorian pose in freefall

Objectivity that inches from the throat
as a dangling velvet worm

I don't fear a rented death

but only in retrospect

The laziest of mutts
channels the precipices that rises as though in front
of the intestinal reading

Do I throw this haunting against the plastic

I presented my counseling to the arms of men (open), where one explored
across the pensum as though they were not fixed in an occupied daylight

I caught my head with my hands and realized how I love my tasteful hyena
rage I see when I am wrong

I love it how my curator says you look like a heartfelt box

He says, I have the guts

DRAWING THE BLIND

Who is asking the question and of what might any adequate
response consist
What is medium

How do I not disturb the limpid surface of the shoal onto
which we throw our glare

I believe in improvisation
I can see now why you row

THE LAND IN THE
STADIUM IS PINK LIFE

For what purpose the city exists
You are my brother (we don't know)

I walked deep into the neighborhoods for a while
until I fell into a swimming pool
full of fairy snow
Wrote a fake name on a napkin
during mercury retrograde
you know

I do not know
I hallucinated you
I do not know
I feel you, and imagine that feeling
as it slides thru the dog

QUEENSBORO PLAZA

Here we slid into the heat

Where sentences come from (me)

I found my intimacy in the midden of the clinic, you don't know
but I know when to remain online

Kept aloft by that drifting heart

What do you know

About the ways of being illuminated gas

Please
          say the buildings

We opened its closed eye

SERENADE

NOTES

"2015 Is Dead" originally appeared in *Too Late*, the limited release chapbook published alongside PIEHOLE's theater production, *Old Paper Houses*, based on the poetry of Bernadette Mayer.

"Eros" begins by quoting Sir Thomas Brown in *Religio medici* (1643).

"Eviction" begins by quoting Isamu Noguchi.

"Expansionism" quotes Dorothea Lasky's "Poem to my Ex-Husband."

"Flower" speaks to Sylvia Plath's, "Stopped Dead."

"Fucking Island" quotes Hiromi Itō's "A Poem for Ueno-San" (trans. Jeffrey Angles).

"The Golden Years" takes its title from the Balthus painting.

"The Raving Ones" borrows from Percy Bysshe Shelley's "The Cloud."

"Rooster Rock" is for Beyer and Garver.

"Water Hour" is a phrase taken from Paul Celan.

ACKNOWLEDGEMENTS

Thank you to the following journals and their editors in which these poems or incarnations of these poems first appeared: *Beecher's Magazine, Cosmonauts Avenue, The Destroyer, FANZINE, HARIBO, Heavy Feather Review, Matter Monthly, No, Dear, Paragraphiti, The Seattle Review, The sensation feelings journal, TAGVVERK*, and *Whiskey Island*.

Thank you to The New School's Creative Writing Program, without which this book wouldn't exist.

Endless gratitude to all the people in my life who guided the formation of this book, knowingly or otherwise. Specifically: Roberto, Justin, Christine, Mark, so many others. Especially you, Moody.

And a tearful thank you, above all, to Mathias Svalina, Zachary Schomburg, Hajara Quinn, Drew Scott Swenhaugen, and everyone else at Octopus Books, for giving *Serenade* a home, and injecting it with energy I never realized possible.

YOUR DEODORANT SMELLS NICE
I'D LIKE TO GET TO KNOW YOU
YOU'RE DEEP FROZEN LIKE THE ICE

X—RAY SPEX, "GERMFREE ADOLESCENTS"